THE WEIGHT OF AN ELEPHANT

Copyright:

THE WEIGHT OF AN ELEPHANT

Published by Krystal Lee Enterprises (KLE Publishing) Copyright © 2024 by K. Lee All rights reserved.
Please send comments and questions:
Krystal Lee Enterprises
services@KLEPub.com
sales@KLEPub.com

To Reach the Author:
Email: me@authorklee.com
Web: AuthorKLee.com Social Media: @AuthorKLee 770-240-0089 Ext. 1

Printed in the United States of America.

All rights reserved. No part of this book may be reproduced or transmitted in any form or by any means, electronic or mechanical, including photocopying, recording, or any information storage and retrieval system without written permission of the publisher except for brief quotations used in reviews, written specifically for inclusion in a newspaper, blog, magazine, or academic paper.

ISBN: 978-1-945066-58-0

Dedication:

To the many boys and girls who have ever felt ashamed, embarrassed, or humiliated because of the hue of their complexion or the color of their skin, I wrote this book for you!

I had a truth heavy on my heart, like the weight of an elephant, and I had to share this book with you! You are valuable and loved; a rich history is associated with you!

I want to thank my family, friends, and loved ones. I love each and every one of you from the bottom of my heart. To my friend Melvina Washington, thank you for helping inspire aspects of this book!
Love always!

"How's my little angel? Why are you crying?" Her baby says nothing but nods her head. I didn't want to say anything. My mom hugged me and said again, "What's wrong, Angel? Why are you crying?"

"I am not an angel, Mom. I am more like the devil."

"Now you hush, speaking like that. You know that isn't true. What's wrong with you?"

"Somebody called me a black devil today at school."

"Really?"

"Yeah. I also got called 'blacky,' 'tar baby,' 'skillet,' and then I just stopped listening. They said I wasn't pretty, Mom."

"Oh baby, children can be so mean. I just hate racism. They don't understand what they don't understand."

"They ain't racist, Mom. These children are black, just like me." Her mom shakes her head because the names and situations her daughter is in today weren't different for her growing up either.

"Why do they have to be mean and call me names? I don't say anything; I just stay in the back of the class and try to cry in peace. But there is no peace. They come by my desk, pull my hair, point at me laughing, calling me "blacky" and "night crawler" because of my hair.

"You just have to ignore children that talk like that." My mom gave me another hug, but the comments still hurt my feelings.

Moments later, in walks my brother, and he says, "Yeah, you gotta get used to people calling you names. I hear it all the time. Tar juice, black bean, black night, or people saying are you blue–black? The one people think is too funny is, Hey James, where did you go? The lights are off, and I cannot see you!"

He starts laughing in an uncomfortable way. "If you can't beat them, join them. Sometimes the comments are funny, and I can't help but laugh with them, so I am not being laughed at."

"But this isn't fair!" I said, and my brother replied, "Life isn't fair, Sis. You gotta get over it and ignore it."

I looked up, and I saw my dad come into the living room, and he said, "Hey, what's going on?"

"Angel is getting called names again," my brother says as he sits on the couch. He nods, sits beside me, and says, "I have something to say."

I look at him and asks, "What do you want to say, Daddy?"

"I want to speak about the elephant in the room."

"What elephant in the room? I don't see an elephant!"

"You're right. It is a saying that means there is a subject that we all overlook about race. If we address it, however, and can talk about it, everyone will feel better after it. Do you want to talk about the elephant in the room?"

"Yes, Dad. I want to see the elephant!"

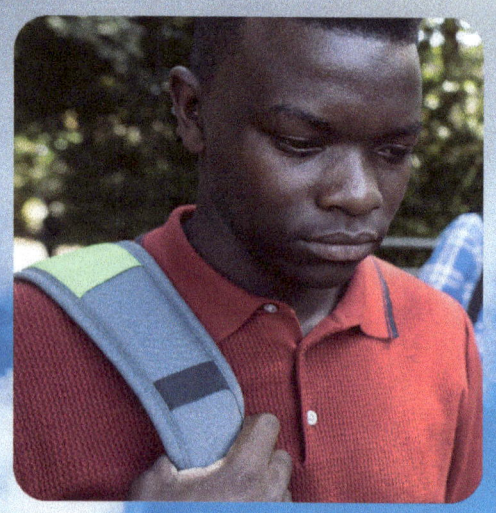

"The elephant is racism, colorism, self-hatred, and slavery. It hasn't been 200 years since our ancestors—for most of us, were brought to this country and spread abroad as slaves. We were sold, taken without our permission, and sold by people who had the same color skin as us and lighter complexions. We were sold because people felt we were less than human, and like the elephant, we were a marvel that held something within us that was so valuable."

"Do you know what makes hunters kill elephants?" My brother said, "No, Dad." My dad replied, "They kill elephants for their tusks, which are their teeth, harvesting them for ivory. And just like that elephant, you have something that other people want to steal—but don't let them!"

I asked, "What do I have that is worth stealing, Dad?" He replies, "I want you to know something that is as heavy as an elephant on my heart."

"How heavy is the weight of an elephant? Is it as heavy as an airplane? Or as heavy as a train?"

"Is it as heavy as a Tsunami rushing through windows sinking floors?" He replies, "Or is it heavy because it can change everything? "

"Really, like what?"

"Like, change you from a caterpillar to a butterfly! Or take you from a tadpole to a frog! Like an ugly duckling changed to a beautiful white and clean swan. Shifted from spotted knowledge to a crystal-clear appearance."

"You gotta tell me, what do you want to say?"

"I want to say that you are not a shade or a color in the crayon box. You are a child for whom so many have prayed. You are beautiful no matter your skin hue—we are all brown if only people knew."

"You are loved no matter your actions. Born more than a slave. You have rich blood, powerful genes, and an incredible story. I must tell the world about how you were scattered to the North, East, South, and the West. To someday be brought to a land that you will never leave. Given to you as a gift from Yah, God above."

"You are the salt of the earth, a jewel in His crown that He sent down to be a light to the world. Shine bright! Never stop smiling. Share your gifts with the world, and never forget your story and calling. You were born beautiful, pigment-rich, sun-kissed. You are my child, the great-grandchild of brave people who believe in you."

"Don't believe that you are nothing because there are people who have already died for you, who know you are something! Yashua gave his life so that He may save the world. But did you know that it all started because of you? You are part of a royal priesthood, a princess, and you are a prince. You don't have to play dress up; this is in your DNA makeup!"

"You are born beautiful! Love your skin, love your smile, enjoy the air you breathe and the story you tell. Be like the elephant: strong, bold, and beautiful. Know that your life story is beau-ti-ful. Your skin is a testament to how God loves you, and your Mom and I do too!"

"We are a family born and called for a purpose, and I will continue to tell you about your story. Never forget who you are and know that how you live is for his Glory!"

Having this conversation with our children can reveal the elephant in the room. Racism is real, but even more so is colorism and the ideals we have formed about those who have a darker complexion. These reservations we have as a culture and the world around us are linked to trauma and real-life events that help us to make decisions to intentionally avoid befriending and even starting families with people of particular complexions.

I want to encourage us all. As we find our balance in knowing who we are and what makes us valuable, we can make the weight of the elephant so light we can jump through the air with change. It doesn't remove the stigma that some people will see, but it will rebuild in us a vision of our beauty and purpose.

True and divine beauty is more than skin deep. It is our heart, mind, and intention to treat all people with value as designed.

Dr. Lee has authored over thirty books across more than seven genres: adult, children, youth fiction, self-help, spiritual growth, novels, business, and empowerment to help people in their most profound times of need.

She is also passionate about coaching programs WAE Process (Write Anything Easily), Embrace Your Crown, Turn Key Solution for Small and New Businesses, and The Lesson for Youth and Teenagers.

- Connect with me using the QR or visit
- AuthorKLee.com
- Social sites with the handle: AuthorKLee

Get Published with KLE Publishing!

If you need a ghostwriter, editor, or want to publish a book visit KLEPub.com or call 770-240-0089 Ext. 1

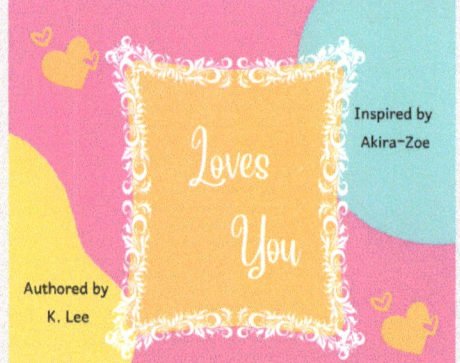

Order More Books Today!

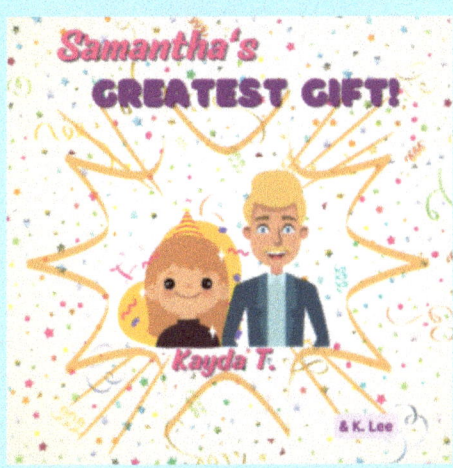

If you need a ghostwriter, editor, or want to publish a book visit KLEPub.com or call 770-240-0089 Ext. 1

www.ingramcontent.com/pod-product-compliance
Lightning Source LLC
Chambersburg PA
CBHW040007080526
44586CB00027B/2909